BENDING
THE
UNIVERSE

BENDING *THE* **UNIVERSE**

Andrews McMeel Publishing
a division of Andrews McMeel Universal
1130 Walnut Street, Kansas City, Missouri 64106

www.andrewsmcmeel.com

18 19 20 21 22 BVG 10 9 8 7 6 5 4 3 2 1

ISBN: 978-1-4494-9394-3

Library of Congress Control Number: 2017959219

Original design & cover by Justin Wetch

Editor: Patty Rice
Production Editor: David Shaw
Production Manager: Cliff Koehler

ATTENTION: SCHOOLS AND BUSINESSES
Andrews McMeel books are available at quantity discounts with bulk purchase for educational, business, or sales promotional use. For information, please e-mail the Andrews McMeel Publishing Special Sales Department: specialsales@amuniversal.com.

BENDING THE UNIVERSE

Justin Wetch

Andrews McMeel
PUBLISHING®

DEDICATION

Dedicated to my friends and family.
Without you, I would have nothing to say.

Special thanks to Malachi Paulsen, who drew the incredible
pencil sketches in this book by hand. His extraordinary
talents and perfectionist work ethic have made this book
so much better than I could ever have dreamed it could be.
Special thanks also to Jovell Rennie for the author photo.

Art is the breath of life.

We are born with the knowledge of breathing. Don't let
the world stop you and teach you not to breathe.

CONTENTS (SECTIONS)

PREFACE

Hello, I am Justin Wetch, a poet, writer, musician,
and photographer from Alaska.

These are my poems. They are the result of five years
of writing my heart out. Please treat them kindly.

There are five sections in this book, each composed of twenty poems.

The sections are Society, Love, Life, Personal, and Nature.

These poems are completely honest. They are 20,000
words in all, and I have given my best effort to make
them the best I could possibly make them.

I hope you enjoy them.

This book was originally self-published in December 2016. It was
published by Andrews McMeel Publishing in spring 2018.

If you're going to distribute these poems, whether online
or otherwise, please attribute them to me. Thank you.

section one

society

SECTION I: SOCIETY

CONTENTS:

There is no change within a society that
does not begin within an individual.

DIVERSITY

Sunlight shines behind a church steeple,
The courtyard filled with diverse people.
But skin color and differences drive us apart,
Our world is afflicted, and it's time for a new start.
Fear of our differences drives us to action,
We could have peace, but choose overreaction.
Our differences are as minor as Pepsi versus Coke,
But they get stronger over time like a piece of oak.
We're split up, as if on separate teams,
Picking winners and losers like cheating at card games.
We judge and discriminate based on the color of skin,
We preach love, but treat diversity as a sin.
Ignorance is a cancer slowly killing our conscience
Eating away at fading chances of gaining tolerance.
I envision a utopia where people are free;
Where nobody is judged based on beliefs or creed.
A diverse city embracing diversity,
Mutual respect bringing an end to animosity.
We may be different, but we have more in common;
Let Martin Luther King's dream never be forgotten.

THE FIRE'S STILL BURNING

The country's gone gay and half of 'em aint happy
Floods in Texas, drought in Silicon Valley
We didn't start the fire but it still burns the youth
Confederate flag's now a symbol of hate groups
Young kids in basements proclaiming they're savages
Police brutality has become the accepted average
Greece is bankrupt, China has all the money
America's just one giant entertainment junkie
Indoctrination, not education, never read between the lines
The future's a dead end and we didn't see the signs
Russia's bringing us back to the brink of cold war
ISIS on the rise, what were the middle east wars for?
Apple's making a watch and the NSA watches your life
130 people bombed in the city of lights
Yeezy for president and Trump's in the lead
140 characters is the most this generation reads
Children who don't fit in boxes are put on meds
Our nation's youth don't see a good future ahead
Ancestors fought for freedom but these kids aint free
Decades of debt for a piece of paper that says 'degree'
Bruce Jenner's now a woman, Rachel Dolezal's not black
Old white guys screaming 'Let's take our country back!'
The church is preaching sermons but the pulpit's rotted
Persecuting gays but pedophile priests are closeted
U2 gives out an album and America throws a fit
Pixar's in the mind but the whole world is out of it
Global warming is cooking us but we don't care
We didn't start the fire but it's our fault it's still here.

GROWING UP

I remember when hands were for comforting
Before they started going up skirts
I remember when lips were for compliments
Before we kissed until being alone didn't hurt.

Hugs turned to sex
Smiles turned to texts
Candy to cigarettes
Schoolyard races to lottery bets
Mountain Dew to mary jane
Hyper kids pronounced insane
'Cool kids' to twitter fame
Asphalt scrapes to mental pain
Snow angels to angel dust
Show and tell to nudes and lust
Growing up is being so rushed
Hopes and dreams quickly crushed.

Oh, but that's the way it goes
Growing up means growing old
We change, seasons change,
Leaves turn to gold.

Call it nostalgia, call it something else
I just wish for a time less . . . complicated
Call it depression, call it needing help
Life's a game and I'm . . . disenchanted.

Life got hard
Shackled to a plastic card
Always on your guard
Self-worth on report cards
We're psychologically scarred
Disgusted with who we are.
Growing up means living less
Screwing over means success
Crumbling under all the stress;
Expensive outfits just to impress
Another lost soul in a dress.
Let's get real, let me confess
I'd rather die than live with regret.

This is what they call growing up in our generation
You can probably understand my trepidation
Of age and its relentless acceleration
It's a prison with no hope for liberation.

We can't spend life chasing new sensations
Or working behind a desk for some corporation
We have to work for happiness and toleration
Because fixing society is our obligation.

Growing up in a world we didn't ask for
Growing up with a low ceiling and no floor
Growing up when dreaming means declaring war
Maybe if we don't grow up we can learn to live more.

THE COSMIC SOUL

People are often uncomfortable
Seeing the flaws in others;
Once we fixate on one piece
Of who another person is
We want to keep them
Inside that little box
On that imaginary pedestal
Confined to that spotlight.

Oh, she has a beautiful smile
And so she is only seen
As a two-dimensional image
Like a tabloid cover model;
But her third dimension
Remains in the dark;
No one asks of her soul
As if she could exist
As pretty skin
Covering nothing.

Having seen someone as flawless
In a particularly good light
The illusion crumbles
Under the harsh weight of reality.

That's the problem with beauty;
Under the surface of a perfect painting
Remnants of rough drafts
Rough pencil sketches,
Flawed structures, wrong colors
Hold up the facade of perfection
Before the elements turn them to dust.

Nothing is ever as it seems
And we are ill-acquainted
With the full dimensions
Of even those closest to us;
We're just fans of the reflections
We pretend others see.

Saying we truly know someone
Is like claiming to be able
To recite a book by memory
Having only seen the cover.

We look to the stars and cosmos
For unsolved mysteries and intrigue
But there is more inside one human soul
That has never felt the weight
Of human footprints
Than all the territories
And domains of the infinite.

THEN & NOW

I remember the stories an old man used to tell
Of war, and heroes made in battle,
They stormed across Germany and fought evil
Like knights of old attacking a castle.

He used to say how one good man of ours
Was worth a dozen or more of the enemy's;
Brothers at war who would die for each other
Living past death in history's memory.

Earlier today I saw a flame war on twitter—
They fought with weapons of misspelled words,
Their shells were snarky comments, a retweet button,
And a bag full of voraciously vulgar verbs.

This great battle of history, fought on the Internet
Is the legacy for that teenage boy's future son
To follow in his footsteps, to be like his father
He'll start his own twitter war and make sure it's won.

I remember the romance story of my grandfather
He pursued his one love year after year
Won her love and affection with sweet words, kindness,
And he never let the sun set with her in tears.

On Facebook I read the screenshotted flirtations
Of a 25-year-old and his current female fling;
They had no tall tale of loving romance but,
They hooked up in the back of a Burger King.

Are all the great stories already lived out?
Is there nothing left for my generation?
I pray we may find something better than
'Hashtag relationship goals' for inspiration.

FEMME

I heard a rich white woman say
The only glass ceilings women have to deal with
Are the ones they put in their villas.

Of course, she married rich
Or, perhaps I should say, divorced rich
So now she's more than half a man;

But I don't think she had it quite right
Because while I'm enjoying a hearty breakfast
My friend applies makeup society says she needs
To be beautiful; how's that not sexist?
So much media attention on women's bodies
That half of them nearly go anorexic
Trying to live up to photoshopped ideals
That are impossible, but still expected.

Are you comfortable in your own skin?
The automatic answer should be yes
But, no, we live in a society where
We force false ideals and wrongly stress
Ideas that should've died decades ago;
In every way, a woman should be less
Than men, and the most naked she can be
Is when she's getting undressed.

From television to advertising
Women are presented as objects and prizes
We're so tolerant we don't realize it.

Sex sells, and it's cheap but so costly
We don't consider the by-products
Of this cancer on society.

The effects are far-reaching and devastating;
A girl in a room with no self-worth
With slit wrists, blood on a Bill Nye poster
Because society told her science was men's turf;
A girl crying, tears flowing from her eyes
Saying her birth gender was a curse
She would've been the world's best eye doctor
But now she'll try to be eye candy, and that's worse.

The science guy, Mr. President, Renaissance man
Embedded in our very words are these thoughts
Passed down to the next generation without question
It's like a massive cultural blind spot
We give men an education, but women are taught
To define themselves by men, and not
To define themselves by themselves;
Fight for who you are and what you want.

TINDERBOX MINDS

Our minds are tinderboxes
Hungering to be lit aflame
Our stances are paradoxic
Preferring cuts to mental pain

Measured meticulous self-destruction
At least we at last feel something
We turn to the warmth of self-combustion
As the burden of life becomes crushing.

Fire is warm, life is cold
So we extend our aching hands
Toward a spark we once sold
For the price of saying "I can't"

Ankles chained to our expectations
We fall gracelessly on our faces
Accepting our future anticipation:
A hangman's noose, a child's shoelaces.

CHURCH

The music stops and they don't really change,
Because it's easy to tip the balance when nothing hangs.
Emotions run high and promises are made,
Then the rats run quickly from sunlight to shade.

The pulpit is beautifully furnished and bright
But it's rotted in places not seen by the light
Millions suffer from famine and plight
But corrupt shepherds push that out of their sight.

The church is a container for performance and stage
Singers up front who were at last night's beach rave;
A social gathering of self-worship and self-praise—
The widows go hungry but the parking lot's paved!

The 'body of christ' is now a lifeless corpse
Preachers plundering pockets without any remorse
Like a battery disconnected from the source,
It'll be lights out without a change of course.

PREACHING TOLERANCE

With how far science and technology have advanced
You'd think we'd have realized our mistakes and re-stanced;
Ridden ourselves of prejudice, et cetera and not chanced
To once again fall prey to judging at a glance.
So late in history, yet equality still aint here,
Visions of a new Eden have disappeared.
You see, we're hardwired to hate what's different, to mistrust,
To block all rationale and let compassion rust.
But we're better than that, or are we not?
Consider how we join the hate onslaught.
With a dark whisper of sensational doubt
The forces of fear and all their clout
Are so easily twisted, so easily bent
To let out dark feelings and hate up-pent.
Like a blacksmith pounding metal into shape,
Our collective conscious is malleable as duct tape.
When we see someone different from ourselves in some way
Say of a different orientation, maybe lesbian or gay
Should that really be a cause for disgust?
As if simple differences are good cause for distrust.
With the choices someone makes you might not agree,
But that's no excuse to trample on their liberty.
It is an evil thing to judge a person into a box
And excuse our own shortcomings, a hypocritical paradox.
If we stopped concentrating on only our differences,
We would reach different conclusions and different inferences
About the quality of a person based on one single factor;
We need a change toward tolerance to avoid disaster.

THE GIRL DOWN THE STREET

There's this girl who everybody knows
She, as they say, just can't say no
And she grows grass she doesn't mow
Indoors where the leaky water flows.

What a whore, what a tramp;
Society is a vicious rubber stamp,
Labeling and assigning camps,
But love is an illuminating lamp.

Born to broken home without guidance,
Screaming and yelling was her silence;
We've got judging down to a science,
Potential liberators become tyrants.

No one to turn to, nowhere to run,
Lovers she has many, lovers she has none;
Looking down the barrel of a handgun,
She looks at your hatred and decides she's done.

Where did this scenario go wrong?
Let me tell you, it won't take long;
Of course she sought solace in a bong,
When she never felt that she belonged.

Everyone judges the girl down the street,
Throwing stones and tapping out tweets;
No, show love and make your words sweet;
Who let you take God's place in the judge's seat?

LOVE IS DEAD

We've started accepting
A shadow of love
As the real thing;
We've started being content
With the shallows
And never learning to swim.

Making love
Has become 'Netflix and Chill'
While smoking green and popping pills

Sending flowers
Has become sexting emojis
Nobody remembers "taking it slowly"

Quality time
Is a thing of the distant past
We love for a night and nothing lasts

Ballroom dancing
Has become dance floor grinding
O-faces have replaced smiling

We don't connect, we hook up, we
Don't get together, we 'get lucky.'

Kissing in the rain
Is now making out at a beach party
While crossfaded on booze and molly

True intimacy
Before honesty required whiskey
Is only glimpsed when tipsy

Love is dead
And we are each to blame
When we took lighters over wild flame.

Rest in peace
To love, once indescribable,
Now nothing desirable

Love was never perfect
And the past is no golden age
But I can't help but feel
We could do better.

ROME

Rome is filled with gleaming white pillars
Crumbling and cracking from the inside
The cobblestone streets are polished but
Under a mask of perfection, decay hides.

The powerful eat from never-ending feasts
While the farmers grow tired of poverty
The people grow weary of corrupt rule
And dream of an overthrown sovereignty.

Death and gore are brought on a silver platter
Colosseums rise up where blood and pain
Are used to entertain all alike, and truly
The emperor rules, but gluttony reigns.

High, impenetrable walls protect the city
Surely even God could not make them fall
But the gate guards are drunk and merry
And never hear the closing call.

Rome, the world's greatest empire
Assailed the most by internal decay
Rome, victim of a slow-acting poison
For every rise there is a price to pay.

America, the world's greatest empire
Assailed the most by internal decay
America, victim of a slow-acting poison
For every rise there is a price to pay.

Stadiums and TV replace colosseums
News and gossip are a daily drug fix
Our thoughts are the result of the media's
Choices of acceptable topics.

Read the YouTube comments section
And tell me you have hope for the future
See the pain that amuses our world
And tell me you're inspired by this culture.

The scales of justice are tilted by money
Lady liberty will take no more weary souls
We're building walls against ourselves
Black versus white, young versus the old;

A house divided against its own self
Is said to face an inevitable destruction
Democrat, Republican, religion, race
How do we expect this house to function?

Constant warfare makes the nation weary
And for what? For corporate greed and oil
The melting pot has reached a tipping point
Society is nearing an unavoidable boil;

We are on the precipitous peak of society
And here we are faced with two options;
Fall off, as Rome did, accepting decay
Or change paths and fix our problems.

AMERICAN JUSTICE

American justice, pure and infallible
In theory, but the reality is laughable
Funny how the bankers who crashed the economy
Got off scot-free, but note the dichotomy
Between that and a nonviolent drug offender
Whose jail sentence was a life-ender.

Fines for being too poor to pay fines
While the rich pay green to do white lines
Fame equals freedom despite it all
Because the powerful will never fall;
Some lives matter less to the justice system
How many more dead before America listens?

The scales of justice are tilted by money
It's rather ironic but far from funny
The powerful get cuff links, not handcuffs
While prison bars make others' hands rough.
Celebrities get rehab, everyone else gets prison
Our justice system has become a cartoon villain.

CANDLES

A sea of darkness overtakes the place
Pitch dark like looking up into outer space
A hush, a silence spills out abundantly
I breathe in to appreciate the profundity
of this moment.

Suddenly a lone flame appears
A spark, in the shape of a falling tear
It sputters, flashing, uncertain
Before standing strong and determined
to exist.

A similar sputter, and now there are two
The first did not shrink, it even grew
Now another, and another, many flames
Vow to keep the world from being the same
fighting stagnation.

Now the whole world is alight with yellow,
orangish light, a field, a meadow
celebrating the existence of this thing
This new idea, taking lift, taking wing
into strength.

Like a candle giving its flame to another
Selflessly, spreading light and color
It takes nothing of ourselves to inspire
goodness in others, to speak life and new fire
into existence.

HOW TO TELL IF YOUR REPRESENTATIVE IS OWNED BY A CORPORATION

Have you ever noticed that your elected representative
Coincidentally seems to work for the rich corporations
That gave them money to get elected?

My oh my, what a strange coincidence!
But surely that can't be the case, for that would mean
We are a democracy of dollars, and not the people.

Well, regardless, I have invented an easy test
To use when one desires to determine
Whether one's representative isn't representing.

If you turn on C-SPAN to watch a voting session
And your congressman is constantly looking over
Their shoulder, like a dog looking for their owner,

If they seem to sweat and look generally slimy
Like their conscious is sweating out
From within and onto their skin;

If you notice any of these signs, you can be sure
That your representative is owned
By a rich and powerful corporation.

You might naturally ask, what can I do about this?
Oh, sorry about that, you can't really do anything
But you can watch as your future is bought and sold.

WELCOME TO AMERICA

Welcome to America, check your culture at the door
Speak one language, identify one way, or it's war
Welcome to America, the dream is dead and we're all poor
Religion is dying off, the new church is the store.

Welcome to America, land of the free and the brave
Here lies freedom, the surveillance state sits on its grave
Our population is fat, entertained, and dazed
And we only see blood right after we've shaved.

Welcome to America, a Wall Street Corporation
Where the stockholders are rich and own this nation
Where cubicle preparation masquerades as education
And people of color are guilty by association.

Welcome to America, just kidding, go home!
Immigrants must have Stockholm syndrome
To see these messages of hateful fire and brimstone
And still want to live here against all wisdom.

Welcome to America, where we preserve the environment
But the city environment has a violence requirement
Discriminatory attitudes have come out of retirement
And our generation has a sense of entitlement.

Welcome to America, I've painted a bleak scene
But it's better than pretending our nation is serene
So look closely at what it has come to mean
When we raise the banner of the American dream.

AND SO SHE WEARS BLACK

She swore she was different
Or just odd, at least
While all the other girls wore
Black leggings, Ugg boots,
And a puffy vest, she
Rocked the world's irises
With a neon onesie
And leopard-print glasses.

But that was a while ago
And being different gets tiresome
After a while;
People enjoy the novelty
Like a new TV show
But when a little time passes
Society is all too willing
To become a mold,
Crushing us all into
Identifiable shapes.

The neon onesie was replaced
With a more normal attire
The leopard glasses became contacts;
She wears mostly black now,
Saying that it's the
Absence of color, and
She wears it because
That's exactly what
Society told her to
Be; colorless, bland, don't rock the
Boat, don't stand out.

And so she wears black
Hoping to fade away
Into the darkness.

MILLENNIALS

We are a generation of nostalgia
But also of forging a new path
We are a generation of artists
Of social media sociopaths.

We are the spray-tan generation
Who also won't eat GMOs
Social media picture filters
Have replaced artistic photos.

We want gluten-free bread
And products responsibly sourced
But when it comes to drugs
Well, it can't be helped, of course.

Our entire lives are stages
And we constantly perform
Each one of us is a star
Narcissism is our art form.

We are so public with what's private
Fame, we can't get enough
Yet we want the government
To stay out of our digital stuff.

We are the fast-food generation
Worshipping popular stores like idols
Max out all the options
With a diet coke, check your vitals.

We post our best selves on social media
But want to be loved for who we are
We delete our worst moments
But want the future to read our memoirs.

We are a generation of contradictions
Of casual existential despair
But maybe we can muster the energy
Just maybe—to ironically care.

GLASS RECTANGLE

In a room, sitting in a circle
In my pocket, that glass rectangle;
The circle fades to gray,
The rectangle lights blue.

Pull away from society
Privatize my personality
Humanity causes me anxiety
Quietly leave for sanity.

My appetite for sunlight
Makes me turn off my device
Despite my peers' advice
Strolling long into the moonlight
Waiting for the dark of night
To feel this sole paradise.

Being alone, who remembers that?
Most people these days couldn't last
And let more than one moment pass
While leaving their solidarity intact.

Reach for that glass rectangle
Like a baby with a pacifier, tranquil
Perhaps one day we'll be unable
To even live without this IV, this power cable.

PATRIOTIC

I've been called unpatriotic for criticizing my country
But what's patriotic about pretending everything's lovely?
Society is sick, be honest that illness is ugly
Even an untreated flu can kill slowly and softly.

I would bleed just to keep the red stripes red
And cheer when I hear that democracy has spread
I feel pride when the flag's allegiance is pledged
But look, we're breaking apart like pencil lead.

The United States of America, in decay
Less united and in a state of disarray
Freedom is dying, liberty has already passed away
Our best days are available for replay.

But why do I point this out so bluntly?
Because, quite simply, I love my country.
I won't let it be destroyed abruptly
Even if that means my words get ugly.

A real patriot won't pretend everything is fine
Sit back in an armchair and blissfully recline
While the streets burn I'll point out the signs
And maybe we'll fix this country of mine.

section two

love

SECTION II: LOVE

CONTENTS:

Love is selfless; only attachment is selfish.

YOUR SONG ON THE RADIO

Time machine to the past
Step back a few years
Old feelings, like
Lazarus
Suddenly reappear.

It's your song on the radio
And it's your hand in mine
As this wave crashes over me
Our stars again come unaligned.

Passion, buried alive
in a coffin of struggle
Has dug itself free
Memories, a sharp shovel.

It's your song on the radio
And here I lie afraid;
That if I change the station
I'll lose you as the signal fades.

The illusion of being okay
Pops like a floating bubble;
The winds of life blew too hard,
This house of cards crumbled.

Scratched out of the picture
But the empty space screams your name;
Past demons haunt the present,
Charred wick now fresh aflame.

It's your song on the radio
and only tears now dance;
Your voice doesn't sing along,
Twilight of a dead romance.

PARTNER IN CRIME

I remember those warm summer mornings
Kicking up dust in the back country
In a red truck, speeding along
Whooping, shrieking, laughing,
Just having a good time
You and I
My partner in crime.

Do you remember the time
We snuck into the forest
Beating the sun to wakefulness
And built a fort in a clearing
Swearing we were running away
From society forever?
We said all we needed was each other
And we'd keep this escapade
From everyone else.
Everyone knew that secret, of course
But no one minded much
For such are the ways of love.

I cherish the simplest memories;
Like the time we were playing in a field
And I tripped over an old log;
You knelt over me
To see if I was quite alright.
The sight of your long hair
The way it looked

Like rays of the morning sun;
The way the wind tossed it playfully about
As you looked down in concern at me;
I had never seen something so beautiful
And you so took my breath away
That I couldn't even speak;
That was the first moment I had ever been in love.

That was before things got complicated.
People started teaching us
All the ways that love
Was supposedly so complex
And that simple thing of ours
Was just not enough;
We learned about the dating game
All the rules and the criteria
And love became so similar
To ordering at a restaurant
Choosing and ordering
But those meals were
Never truly satisfying.
So let's forget everything they taught us.
Let's run wild and free
And pursue every breeze
The winds of our hearts
Demand that we be.
Let's throw out the rules
The criteria, the nonsense,
Oh, let us become again
Partners in crime.

ORBIT

Like two stars in the depths of the sky
This gravity is just irresistible
We spin around each other, you and I
When I fell for you, I fell into your orbit.

Our constellation is a beating heart
Two, beating as though they are one
The galaxies would cry if we were to part
If ever we fell out of orbit.

Giving into this gravity is a scary thing
I tried to pull back and to hide
But now I join the song your galaxy sings
I'm falling freely into your orbit.

WHAT I FELL IN LOVE WITH

I fell in love
With the edges of your lips
With your scratchy morning voice
And the detail in your fingertips

I fell in love
With your silly shy smile
With your hair in the sun
And your summery sense of style

You brought me to places
I'd have never thought to go
To a trail near the river
Where the water runs slow;
To a mountain where all we heard
Was our voices' echo;
You showed me inward beauty
That doesn't show in photos.

I fell in love
With more than I could need
With a deep soul
And a face I couldn't leave;
I fell in love—
If I may tell it true;
I fell in love
With every piece of you.

SOMEONE ELSE

I walked up to your door
With roses in hand
Ready to ask
If your heart would be mine;

Might we grow together
In the sunlight of love
Like two oak trees
Standing strong
Against weather and change?

But when I came to your door
Pausing to check again
My appearance
In my reflection
In your window
I froze
Like a blue jay
Who has forgotten
To migrate south
For the winter.

In each other's arms:
The girl I loved
And another man.

The wistful gazes
The romantic dances
The rain kisses
The contented smiles
Everything I wanted
You gave
To someone else.

I dropped the roses
Trampling them
As you did
Our blooming flower;
I left angrily
Without a second glance.

Oh, the pain of reality
I cannot stop loving you
But you've given your heart
To someone else.

Oh, how it destroys me
This simple revelation:
You've given your heart
To someone else.

TO LOVE IS TO LIE

Love is just two people
Plastering perfect masks
On each other's faces;
And it only lasts
Until the masks crack
And the fantasy ends.

Promises of forever
Resonate for seconds
And die with the echo;
Sweet words sprout
But decay with the seasons
Like saccharine fruit.

To love is to lie
Sweetly, then bitterly
Further down the road;
As the knife is pulled out,
Leaving the heart as empty
As it was to begin with.

The most pathetic of lies
Are the ones we tell ourselves,
Desperately clinging to hope;
Namely, that passion
Is more than an illusion, and
Love is more than a lie.

TO LOVE IS TO LIVE

Love starts as a feeling,
But to continue is a choice;
And I find myself choosing you
More and more every day.

Like two flowers
Which begin from separate roots
But entangle and grow as one
We are stronger together.

You make me feel
Like I deserve the world
Even though I have nothing to give
But love and laughter.

When I look into your eyes
It's so easy to forget
What it was like
To stare into life's darkness

When I listen to your laugh
It's so easy to forget
Every pessimistic word I ever said
About love and romance.

REACHING ACROSS THE DISTANCE

I'd die before talking to you again.
No, I mean
I would have to be dying
Before I could muster the courage
To reach out to you
Like a bridge across an ocean
Between two faraway continents
Reaching across the distance
Like a candle
Hoping to illuminate
A universe of darkness.

Once again I've put your number
Into my phone
And all that is left
Is for me to press
The call button,
And just like that
This needle would drop
Into our austere silence
Like a gunshot
Fired
Into a hushed abyss.

But for the thousandth time

I clear it away
Like a flamethrower
Declaring this chance
Of rebuilt bridges
To be so much kindling
Just more fuel
Sacrificed at the altar
Of chance
And possibility.

Are we like two stars in a constellation
Seeming so close
And making so much sense
Yet in reality
We are separated by light-years
And shall never meet?
Except, perhaps
In that sacred space
Between dreams and reality
Called hope.

PARAPHERNALIA

With shaky hands I adjust
The instrument of my addiction
I breathe in, in, in
Eyes fluttering as
The waves of pleasure hit.

My brain sloshes to mush
Hands finally become steady
I see my exhale in the moonlit air
Rolling my head back
In pure release.

You are my drug of choice
I know you're no good for me
And though I swear my lips
Will never touch you again
Here we are, here we are.

Your whispers, like electricity
Flirt with the edges
Of the neurons in my brain
Taking captive my will
Into a vortex of your smile.

Passion drips in the humid air
Like moonlight peeking through
The gaps in the arms of oak trees;
Flittering a monochrome painting
Onto the soft, leaf-ridden floor.

The music stops and the dance dies
Your chemical abandons my brain
And I hold my head in my hands
Regretting, as I do every time
That I have succumbed to your siren song.

As we lie next to one another
I stare into your tresses of hair
And imagine that I could twist them
Into a hangman's noose
And end this cycle forever.

But that thought passes quickly
And I escape through the cracked window
Swearing you off for the thousandth time
But still knowing, deep down inside
I am addicted to your essence.

FOREVER

You see flaws in every face
If you look long enough.

That's why I'm so afraid
Of the word 'forever.'

Forever is long enough
For sunrises to become stale
For fire to become tame
For a favorite song
To become like nails
On a chalkboard;

Forever is long enough
For passion to waste away
Like grapes into raisins
Under the beating sun
Of countless days.

Every promise of 'forever'
Brings with it a tainted air,
A perfume of dishonesty
Reeking of roses wilting
For even beauty has limits
And its seasons.

I don't want to look
—Some day in the future—
Into familiar irises
And find handcuffs
Where I used to see stars.

So I won't take forever
For granted.

Let us love like the spark
Between flint and stone
In reckless abandonment,
Promising no eternities,
But promising only to seek out
Upon each day's sunrise
Something to choose to love
In each other.

MUSE

Blood becomes less blood
Sky becomes less light
Ash becomes oxygen
Mind becomes a metropolis
Where the streets are named after you.

I get lost on these streets
Like I do in your eyes
The back of my hand is lost
To memory in your mind
Be careful not to fall from
On my mind with heels that high;

Brain turns to mush
Tongue turns to a tie
Eyes turn to beacons
Lips turn to ships
Which find each other in this darkness.

In a moment you're my muse
My Aphrodite, a Greek sculpture
Your arms might not be heaven
But they're sure as hell closer
Than here, but like purgatory
Bliss doesn't come without torture;

Two became one
But then one became two
Embrace becomes a standoff
Eden becomes Earth
And perfect unity falls out of sync.

I used to paint my muse from up close
Now I can only admire you from afar
I used to drink from Pirene
Now I pick poison from a bar
My muse, my muse, how did we fall
From what we were to what we are?

THE HEART COLLECTOR

I'd be lying if I said I didn't want you
I'd be lying if I said I didn't wish you were mine
The truth is, you stole my heart from afar
The truth is, you still have it.
You took a piece of me when you left
I had cupid's arrow straight to the heart
When you pulled it out without a care
I said I loved you as I bled out.
Your eyes could make the brightest
Of the brightest diamonds jealous
And your lovely smile
Could melt the hearts of the cold.
I held my arms open to you
I wanted badly your embrace
But you walked on past without a care
As I stood in the wind, alone.
I stood with that pose for a thousand years
I stood, waiting for two to be one
But never did you deign to glance my way.

I froze when fall turned to winter.
A statue, standing against the snow
A monument against what love is
I watched couples walk by on the street
And glance suspiciously at their lovers.
Then spring came at last and I
Finally melted, finally became free
I fell to a fetal pose and lay
There for the whole summer.
I saw you walking past as I lay
There, thinking over my life
A new man at your shoulder.
You pushed him up against a tree
And added another arrow to your collection.
I watched as he fell to the ground
I watched as he tried to rise again;
I realized you were addicted to this art
I realized this was your one true passion.
You had no love for the hearts you stole
You only loved the moment of leaving.
I'd be lying if I said I didn't want you
I'd be lying if I said I didn't wish you were mine
The truth is, you stole my heart from afar
The truth is, I finally took it back.

HIGH ON YOUR PERFUME

Call me obsessed, color me consumed
I've always been the type to notice
The smell of a rose in bloom,
But let me confess, this is new
You've stopped my heart, let it resume
And I, to finish, must tell it true
I'm high on your perfume.

Like a mouse tempted to cheese
An elixir of life that must be tasted
I toss away all fear and unease
And oh, the risk that the trap will spring,
I breathe it in deeply like an autumn breeze;
You locked my attention on yourself,
Took it all; and threw away the keys.

Breathe in, in, in, can't get enough;
Excuse me if I linger a second longer . . .
Eyes gloss over with a whiff of lust,
You bite your lip, I can't resist;
We close our eyes, we do, we must;
Now that I've tasted who you are
I'm addicted, I can't get enough.

CHOICE

To truly love someone
with more than fleeting attraction
means consciously choosing
and committing to them,
putting in the work
to make it last.

A FOOL'S ODE TO HIS LOVE

I cannot help but say
That I have fallen in love with you.

Perhaps it was your voice,
Whispers which hinted of music;
Or the way your eyes sparkled
When you spoke of passion;
Of my endearment to you,
I am witless of the origin.

I found a night's sky full of stars
In your cinematic eyes
And heard a symphony
In your laughter.

Your lips are like a cherry
Begging to be tasted
And to caress your face
Is to feel sunlight.
You are a ray of sunshine
In this dark world;
While the day is young
I must suntan.

LOVE & LOGIC

In math and science, we learn everything has a reason
It's physics, it's gravity, it's a reaction going to completion
But I cannot divine, cannot figure out one thing
The reasons behind love; surely it must be something!
There are others with pretty eyes, but I like yours best
But why? Perhaps just because they reflect
The moon and stars with such timeless ferocity
Or our own hearts in orbit with increasing velocity
There are seven billion faces smiling in as many ways
But if I don't see yours, I consider it a wasted day.

What is it about you that's so irreplaceable?
You're an original masterpiece, the signature unmistakable.
In love, it seems every heart has its own locked door
And each of us has a key, but we know not which one it's for
Perhaps that explains the feeling I feel about you;
Perhaps that is why it is so impossible to subdue
My relentless adoration for the person I see
Even though the reasons are buried in my psyche
But maybe love doesn't need reasons or a list sorted,
Maybe it is what it is, and the reasons why aren't important.

ANESTHETIC

Mind blurred by the painkiller I was on
Didn't even realize open heart surgery was happening
But suddenly I've snapped to awareness
And now I feel everything.

You were the anesthetic
That dulled life's pain
But you left a void in my consciousness
And now nothing's the same.

Pulse has gone to a flat line
I'm screaming but no one hears me
Vision fades to black on black on black
Mental burns to the third degree.

Everything's vivid and burning
Bereft of the dullness that kept me
My anesthetic has worn off
Your place in my mind is empty.

WRITE YOUR NAME

I came up with a new reason
To write your name today
I plagiarized each letter
From a love note you wrote me.
The scent of ink was sacred to me
In that relapsed moment . . .
For a minute I could pretend
The paper reminded me of your skin;
I could pretend the glimmering ink
Was the moonlit lake
Of our summer night.
But the pretending crumpled with paper
And I threw us into the trash can
For the bridge between us is long burned
And it's time I accepted that.

COLORS

I used to see a sunset
And marvel at its beauty
The sight of the sun dancing down
Was enough for me.

I used to sigh with contentment
At the taste of a fresh grape
And smile at the colorful leaves
On the ground, with their many shapes.

But then I looked into your eyes
And I was colorblind no more
With the perspective you gave me
Your voice became my life's musical score.

I could see a whole new color, it seemed
The primary three, and this new fourth color
That I couldn't quite pin down, but around you
Drab gray became vibrant summer.

We watched the sunset together again
For the umpteenth time, it didn't dismay
But when I looked for you, you had disappeared
I had to stop searching as last light faded away.

When I awoke the next morning,
Something had gone terribly wrong.
The sunrise was dull and disappointing
And the birds sang a most discordant song.

When you left, you left a void
In my perspective of the world
Leaving me to see everything
Nasty, distorted, and curled.

It was the same as it had been at the start
Before you taught me to see a new way
But having tasted the finest of life
The old way wouldn't do, this wasn't okay.

Like looking at the sun, recovery takes time
And time is a tedious medicine
Looking back, I began to wonder
If your love was ever genuine.

But it was for the best, I'm now quite sure
I learned and experienced new things
And yes, it does sometimes still feel
Like your leaving chopped off my wings . . .

I used to see a sunset
And marvel at its beauty
The sight of the sun dancing down
Was enough for me.

Now I look at a sunset
And nearly smile at its beauty
The sight of the sun dancing down
Is almost enough for me.

LITHIUM

Manic, intense highs
Followed by horrific, terrible lows
Strobing between blinding light
And blind darkness.

This bipolarity encapsulates her love;
Sometimes we are a storybook romance
And sometimes a vendetta of revenge.

Sometimes it feels like even if
Every inch of my skin was touching yours
I still wouldn't be close enough to you.

And other times even if we were
On opposite ends of the globe
I would still feel too close to you.

Have you ever wanted to love someone so powerfully
So desperately, so obsessively
That they destroy who you are as a person?
That the fabric of your life is burned to a crisp
by the unending intensity of it all . . .

Those are the highs.
In those times, her love spreads a silly stuporous smile
Across my canvas of a face
And I couldn't be higher.
But when you go too high, you run out of oxygen.

Love gives the best of highs
But also the worst of hangovers.

When vision blurs
And indecision surges
It's like looking into the black abyss of space
From the surface of the sun
The sheer light behind you
Masks the stars ahead
And everything is blackness.

Even simple things are joyless
And our love
Which once lit up every corner of the universe
Now barely keeps dying embers aglow.

To treat this bipolarity, the doctors prescribed Lithium.
Lithium is a woman of steady goodness
She knows nothing of mountains or valleys
Only flat, endless plains
Which little effort is required to move through
But there are no captivating views.

My first love wore vibrant colors at times
And funeral dresses at others
Lithium wears only a calming gray
And knows nothing of frowns
Only a perpetual smile.

She is always calm
And would never suggest silly things
Like cliff diving or random midnight drives . . .
Our calendars are planned and always followed through
And she always thinks three steps ahead.

Every Sunday after church
We eat at the same café
She orders the same salad and black coffee
And I order a trip down memory lane
To a time with my first love
When I was so caught up in her
That I forgot to eat for two days . . .

She talks of marriage now
We go so well together, she says,
And we never, ever clash!
We never make offensive jokes
Or improvise our lines
But hey, we're happy, aren't we?
Aren't we?

So why do I want to go off my meds?
When Lithium leaves her night-light on
—she can never sleep without it, she says—
I only long for darkness.
What is this sickness within me
That longs to be burned to ashes by a fierce passion
And hates this peace?
This dreadful, meaningless, horrible, good calmness.

So in the middle of the night
I awaken in a cold sweat
And without a plan, leaving everything behind
I flee to a foreign city
Where I don't even speak the language
Where the doctors don't know my name
Where the Lithium will soon wear off
And I will soon be free again.

I don't want safety or guarantees—
I want a life worth living.
I want to jump off a skyscraper
And fashion a parachute on the way down
Out of my fears and trepidations
Because sometimes survival
Isn't the most important thing
And surviving
Isn't the same as living.

With arms opened wide I await
The oncoming storm
That wonderful, violent, colorful storm
It may destroy every particle of me
But at least I'll feel alive and free.

Perhaps these are the words
Of someone who learned to love passionately;
Or perhaps these are the last words
Of a junkie who couldn't get high enough.

section three

life

SECTION III: LIFE

CONTENTS:

What a beautiful, relentlessly haunting thing;
the space between hope and reality.

DUST ON THIS PIANO

In the attic of this old house,
Up the creaky, torn carpet stairs;
I draw open the curtains;
Light permeates the air.

My eyes squint as the sun
Announces its presence with a shout.
Here, packed away in cardboard boxes;
Are dreams that never panned out.

Dust settles in the sun's rays
Calmly on a mute piano
A paintbrush's tip lies dried up
No mark on this canvas but shadow.

A paper lies on an old wooden desk
And on it, a pencil with broken lead.
A glass of lukewarm water sits
Next to half a piece of rotted bread.

I have to ask, what happened here?
With a teardrop-stained mirror, broken;
So much wasted potential—
A door locked, but left open.

Perhaps here I see the crime scene
Where someone was given a toxin
Or suffocated until all they had
To breathe with was oxygen.

I see the seat where Mozart was killed
Crushed by this pile of textbooks.
And here, Da Vinci bled to death
Cut by this stack of bills, it looks.

So, why this massacre of genius?
Perhaps under so much pressure
Only a cog in the machine is made
Not always some diamond treasure.

It is such a pity how some people
Are dead long before their hearts stop beating.
This old man died at twenty-five
When life told him to stop dreaming.

Perhaps it is not too late for me
To escape this endless loop
Maybe those who live past death
Are the ones who continued to hope.

I wipe the dust off this piano
Watch it flee away, escaping
As I push down on this untuned key
I feel a life worth living awaiting.

EMPTY WEALTH

Ten thousand-dollar suit
Two thousand-dollar shoes
Boasting of immense wealth
But never knowing what's true.

Matching Rolex watches
Not happy after all
Bought a huge new mansion
With gold-plated walls.

A garage full of Lamborghinis
Can't fill an empty heart
Sometimes even the rich
Wish for a fresh start.

A pocket full of cash
Nothing left to spend it on
Already bought the world
Done everything that's wrong.

People say they're his friend
But how could he ever be sure?
When you leave a trail of dollar bills
You can't be sure your loves are pure.

What use is it, really
To take your millions to the grave
When instead of living life
You've become your own slave?

This is the life of a millionaire
A glass so full it's empty
A hole that can't be filled
By a new Mercedes or a Bentley.

Nothing he can't have
Except for what he wants
A shadow of the real thing
A phantom desire still haunts

He'd willingly go poor
Just to have a real friend;
You can have the whole world,
But your world will have to end.

We believe that more is better
But sometimes less is more
Sometimes endless wealth is empty
A pot of gold with a trap door.

Because if you've gained everything
It becomes its own prison walls
Don't lose what matters most
To get what doesn't matter at all.

RETIREMENT

They give us eighteen years
To figure out how to spend our lives;
We're pushed toward high-paying careers
At the cost of letting our dreams die.

They say it'll all be worth it
When you finally get to retire
When you run out of things
To shoot for, to aspire.

Is it really worth it
To spend all these years
Navigating a maze of mirrors
Building someone else's empire
Just so that our last decade
When our bodies have already decayed
Will at last be peaceful?

Let us hold a funeral for happiness
Let us mourn the death of joy
Crunching corporate numbers all day
Darkens our inner light till it's destroyed.

Does it have to be this way?
Is this the only available path?
It's all so confusing and nonsensical
Like those formulas in math.

I want my life to be more
Than a dollar figure amount
Or the statistics in my bank account;
I want to live a life
Where retirement isn't necessary,
Where all my years are satisfactory.
I won't live for life's last decade.

DREAMING

I remember sitting in bed, as a child
Looking up at the ceiling
I couldn't sleep, of course,
And so set about to thinking
I wondered, what are dreams made of?
Are they stardust and galaxies?
Are they the tendrils of existence
Reaching inward from eternity?

I didn't know, and really, still don't.
All I knew and know is what it's like
When reality loses its hardened grasp
On perception, as dullness begins to die
As the body begins to be motionless
And the truth comes out as we lie
Silently for hours, flying into that
Far away, beautiful landscape beyond here.

Dreaming with eyes closed to the world
But this is no inhibition to seeing
A world somehow beyond this one
Frail, crumbling, loose, and fleeting;
An oddball splattering of paints
Mixed from real life and something else,
They ooze together on this canvas and so die
To come alive in some other realm.

Light whirls in eight-dimensional streams
Darkness is contained in a crystal hidden
Behind our eyes to protect our innermost dreams
From the ease of destruction of all new things;
Dreams flutter and leave behind a trace
As eyes match the motion and slowly open—
Briefly, magic and Earth are both in place;
I lament the sadness of being awoken.

MUSIC THEORY (OF LIFE)

Life is a decrescendo until death
With many flats
And few rests
Ending in a full stop

Modulating into madness
Suspension into sadness
Vibrato relieving the flatness
Moonlit sonata against the blackness

Chords of misery
Triads of despair
Bars of brokenness
Coalescing in crescendos
Motifs of mystery
Transposing terribly
Into dark dissonance

Whole notes of pain
Boredom and darkness
Half notes of light
Flirting and romance
Quarter notes of peace
Quiet and simplicity

What is life, if not a song
Made of imperfect melodies
And it ends before too long
With cruelty in great quantity

But perhaps it's not all dark
Nor does light come without energy
Perhaps perspectives make their mark
And put dissonance into harmony.

AS JOY DWINDLES WITH THE YEARS

Why do the holidays
Lose their charm over the years?
Why does Christmas
Not seem like Christmas anymore?
These special days
Lose their magic
With the passing of time.

It flows from us
Betraying us
For the next generation.
I envy the sparkle
In their young eyes
As they are still enchanted
By fairies, santa, and
A host of joyful lies.

I recall the way
A present used to feel
Like a box of endless mystery
In my hands;
My own portal
To a world
Of infinite possibility
Of infinite amazement.

Now I get things I need
Instead of fuel for the imagination;
—Legos used to call my mind
To hours of new adventures
Building spaceships and skyscrapers
Rising high above that stained carpet
Into the cosmos above
Beyond mere reality—

Now here's some flavored coffee
To work harder with
And watch the hours pass by
Ever faster and faster.

What is it about growing older
That bites venomously
Into the neck of hope?

As joy dwindles with the years
I wistfully recall
When the Christmas tree
Looked ten feet tall
And the presents under it
Seemed endless
And more
Than mere wrapping paper.

Kiss goodbye to wonder, once so near;
Must joy dwindle so with the years?

HIDING FROM SILENCE

Blaring loud music
Flipping through channels
Insanity, excuse it
Anything to avoid silence

Who's dating whom?
Celebrities and gossip
Like animals at a zoo
We are so predictable.

Distraction after distraction
To keep real thoughts away
Lulling ourselves into inaction
We talk so much yet we have nothing to say.

Mathematical formulas
couldn't quantify the feeling
The inevitability of death
And the slowness of mental healing.

We hide from silence
For it forces us to think
Where our lives are going
and what makes us distinct.

So stop hiding from silence
Introspection is no evil thing
Listen to your heart and self
Silence is good, though it stings.

CLEARING THE SCOREBOARD

It's all too easy to start keeping score
Of those who hurt you, and do you wrong
It's so easy to say someone owes you
To hold a grudge for ever so long.

These scoreboards are heavy and hard
To carry around on your back
It's such a powerful inner monster
Who sees every slight as an attack.

It sounds simple, but is harder than it looks
Clear the scoreboard, don't keep count
Of the ways people have wronged you
Clear their debts, reset their account.

Few good things have ever come freely
Clearing the scoreboard, while a task not easy
Leads to a path of peaceful coexistence
If you learn to forgive often and completely.

FROSTBITE

There is one feeling
That all humankind
Cannot bear to feel.

That is the feeling
Of being alone.

Perhaps it developed
To keep ancient cavemen
From wandering too far
From the safety of numbers;
Or perhaps it arose
From the memories of stardust
Separated by parsecs
Which form our earthly shells.

In any case, the feeling beckons
When sleepy eyes jolt open
And for just a moment you feel
Like the last person on earth.

The universe—a cavern
Too big to return an echo—

The stars stare back
In that deep,
Soul-shattering blackness
And from the depths of existence

Comes a cruel, icy wind
Raising the hairs
On the back of your neck
And suddenly it feels
Like you're walking a tightrope
Over that endless abyss
On one sad, fraying, thin
Violin string.

It mocks everything
You could hold dear—
Money, fame, love
It wilts like a rose
Thrown suddenly
Into outer space.
To understand this
Of human nature
Is to understand
Every human action;

Every performance
Every deed
Every poetic love
Is this, and only this:
We can't bear
The emotional frostbite
Of being alone.

DIETARY CONSIDERATIONS

You are what you eat
Too much and you become obese
Need energy? Caffeine release
Eat right to avoid disease.

So what do you feed your spirit?
Do you exercise your mind?
Do you push creativity to the limits
Make time for self-reflection, look inside?

Are you balanced and healthy?
Do you manage your diet correctly?
Is your spirit fat and sweaty?
Is your mind sick and deathly?

Watch what you eat
Meditation is like good coffee
Dietary considerations are incomplete
If you're only concerned for your body.

MONUMENTS OF INK

Photographs have an odd way of lying.
Or perhaps they merely present
The past truths we would rather forget—
Laying them to rest at the grave of memories
Once cherished in the times they lived.

These colorful polaroids
Are like magical portals
Leading to places, emotions, and people
Who had slipped into the midst of the forgotten,
Into the odd ether of willful omittance.

They scream greetings from their frozen afterlife
Imposing their awkward smiles,
Their connections between wayward souls
Which have long since snapped
And shattered like cursed mirrors.

This piece of inked paper stands a colossus
A monument to a string of moments once dear;
The only surviving testament to a time
When these background bridges remained unburned,
Before they became so much unswept rubble.

In vain I try to jump into the photo
To create again a time so simple
That a piece of paper might encapsulate it
From the erosive winds and waves of time
Which bring even the greatest of loves to a grave of dust.

MONUMENTS OF PIXELS & LIGHT

I never thought
That someone I once saw
So vividly, before my very eyes
Would one day disappear
Into a mediocre monument
Of pixels and squares of light;
A poor representation of reality.

This blurry selfie
Is all that connects me
To these past memories;
It is the only evidence
That the light of our sun
Once fell on both
Our cloudless faces
One summer day.

The only remnants
Of our myriad conversations
Are occasional updates
Like highway markers
On the road of life;
Or videos
Shared with a laughing emoji
Like the ones
We used to laugh at
Together.

It is like seeing an apparition
In the desert;
It looks so real
But is a trick of the light,
For I am certain
That this prison of pixels and dots
Could not contain
The person I once knew
Even though for now
It appears to.

NEWTON'S THIRD LAW OF EMOTION

I am convinced that the laws of nature
Which govern the universe
Govern human beings equally so.

What comes up must go down;
For every action there is
An equal and opposite one.

These universal truths
Are imbedded within ourselves
And imbue our psychology.

There is no comedic genius
Who did not grow up with pain
There is no great artist
Who did not grow up with the same.

One must fear to lose the present moment
To capture it beautifully in photography
One must fear life to be flavorless
To be a chef who cooks flawlessly.

As artists, we create the beauty
We are too afraid to live out
And search, but always fall just shy
Of finding what life is about.

LIFE IS PROFOUNDLY SAD

Life is profoundly sad.
I swear that for every sunny day
Without a care in the world
And every breezy afternoon
Where the wind soothes;
The cost must be paid;
And the price is counted
In sleepless nights
Spent looking at the ceiling
Searching in those etched patterns
For some sort of adhesive
To glue together the broken pieces
Of a soul crushed
By the weight of the fact that
Life is profoundly sad.

DISCOVERING MENTAL INJURIES

Have you ever looked at your hands
And found a mysterious cut or bruise?
You don't remember getting it
But the evidence is clearly there.
Maybe you discover it
When using hand sanitizer;
It stings, and hurts sharply,
Stealing space in your consciousness.

I've been wondering lately
If the same thing exists for the mind.
Maybe you're just sitting in your room
Sketching absentmindedly,
Or just sitting there, quietly
Thinking about life's happenings,
And you stumble upon an injury
You didn't know you had.

Something someone said
That you pretended didn't hurt
Or something you wanted to say
But didn't have the courage to
Anything gnawing at your mind
Creating a cystic scar;
Perhaps the sound of a certain voice
Is what calls it to your attention.

Discovering mental injuries
I begin to wonder cautiously
What if they're infected?
What if this is a slow death?
Maybe awareness is all we have
And true treatment is impossible . . .
I guess I'll just bring a band-aid
And hope these mental injuries heal.

POSTMODERN ANGST

Love is the poetry of the stars
The wind is the breath of the earth
To never become who you are
Or to change at all, which is worse?

To find a love you must someday lose
Or to deny it to never feel loss
Remain half or lose half, we must choose
Is the value of love worth its cost?

We are a handful of dust in God's image
Before we return again to dusty grave
Life isn't a war, it's a scrimmage
A hyphen between two dates.

At any second we could be writing
Our biography's very last page
And not even realize it, how exciting—
We're just actors on life's stage.

MIDNIGHT

Midnight is the cruelest of hours, breeding
Dark thoughts out of the blackness, freeing
Despair from the prison of happiness, meeting
Anxiety and fear in a treacherous alley, waiting
To bring a murderous end to hope before morning.

Fate is the cruelest of masters, taking
Life when it pleases or at random, handing
Rigged decks to whom it pleases, cheating
All alike and none the wiser, taking
Everything away from those with nothing.

Hope is a foolish disaster, ending
All realism and rationality, lying
Always promising too much, trying
To blunt the painfulness of life, muting
Dark thoughts and catalysts for weeping.

Sadness is the cruelest of emotions, crying
Deep sobs into the canyons of the mind, singing
Broken songs of torment and death, sending
Echoes at random into the future, requiring
All happiness to be punctuated with mourning.

Time is the cruelest of physicians, healing
All wounds, but always slowly, looping
A surgical needle through the mind's flesh, experiencing
Torment again and again, repeating
Until anesthetics bring an end to feeling.

GOODBYE

You're saying something to me
But I can't pay any attention
My eyes are locked onto our hands, together
Thinking of everything I forgot to mention.

You're leaving, oh yes I know, you keep saying so
You say we'll be reunited, but that's just not enough
I know this is hard for you too, but you keep saying
To hold onto your memory and never give up.

You say you left some boxes full
Of things I might need while you're gone
Some pots and pans and a recipe book
And oh, an antique glass chess pawn.

You've got to go, the boarding call sounds
But symphonies play sad melodies in my head
I want to take this time to say goodbye
But I can't, I just can't, so I'll just nod instead.

You're boarded and gone and soon far away
I burst into tears, head in my hands
I know you'll be happier, sure,
Off to leave some footprints in new sands,

But I never got to say that I loved you,
Never got to hug you one last time and say goodbye
Never got one last time in the park
To watch the stars fade into sunrise.

You're gone forever, out of my life
I know your spirit has gone away to fly
I'm so sorry I didn't have the courage
To say I loved you, to say goodbye.

THE WAVE

Life is the ups and downs of a wave
Sadness, joy, cycles of years and days
With different depths and unpredictable frequency
Everything comes and goes in seasons and sequences
From the moment the lightwave first hits the leaf
To the moment the wind knocks it down from the tree.

Good news, "I love you's," lies and truths
Are all communicated when the soundwaves move.
Every atom held together by electron waves
The waves of mystery holding together time and space
From the moment a baby opens eyes and takes breath
Till a soul is taken from us by the cruelty of death.

The brain waves of a thought, a dance, a kiss
Emotional heights, plunging into the abyss
The waves of the ocean echoing upon the shore
The waves of blood shed in scores in war
History repeats itself and so do our lives
Future set in stone, none of us survive.

Everything is connected, all part of a whole
Every word from different depths of the same soul
Ups and downs, what goes around comes around
As strands of future and past come unwound
Life is more than just death's wicked countdown
Life is a wave—so swim, surf, or drown.

A MAN IN THE RAIN

There is an old man walking in the rain
On this empty road as the leaves fall
His skin is wrinkled, his glasses thick;
he carries an umbrella, but doesn't use it
He hobbles along, using it as a cane
Without a care as to the drizzling shower
of water coming from up above.

He finds an old wooden bench, and sits heavily
Lowering himself gently as it creaks in protest
He exhales laboriously and settles in,
His breath visible in the chilly autumn air
He sets the umbrella down beside him
In her place, where she used to sit.
He holds his head in his hands, and shudders.

Tears run among their relatives, the rain
And streak through every crack in his face
Falling slowly toward his heart
Or, rather, the half of it still remaining
In his chest, the other half not beating back
In time from across that old bench
The way it used to, time ago.

His joints and bones ache from the cold
But he doesn't even notice, or doesn't care
Why would he, when he stands, incomplete
His old eyes drowning under waves of despair;

He caresses the empty seat slowly, trying
To recall his most precious of memories;
But her face is taken from him once more.

His Italian accent still shows through a bit
When he mumbles a bit from her favorite song,
But he can't finish this serenade, he collapses
Into a puddle of sadness beyond language
Crying bitter, bitter tears onto the pavement
He has nothing, nothing left at all
Nothing, nothing left but shattering tears.

A car screeches by, running through a puddle
Sending a wave of muck cascading over him
But it's no different from the way life has been
To him ever since that one wretched day . . .
He sees the wilted rose she had once proudly
Watered and been sunshine to, or perhaps he
Only sees his own reflection in a puddle, dying.

There is an old man, walking in the rain
With a story to tell but nothing left to say
He carries an umbrella, only a walking stick
A crutch, to keep him further from the world;
He's alone, waiting, vacillating indecisively
Between trying to glue himself back together
Or letting go of a heart broken apart.

Midnight is an hour only
criminals and artists can
fully appreciate

section four

personal

SECTION IV: PERSONAL

CONTENTS:

What a cruel irony it is, that we get to choose
our thoughts but not our feelings.

PASSPORT

These pages are filled with the places I've been
The beliefs I've changed and the sins I've sinned
The past versions of myself, each leaving their mark
In the ridges of my brain and veins of my heart

Changing musical tastes, changing features of my face
Changing viewpoints, different breezes to chase

Stamped with scars and troubling times
Soiled with dirt and splotches of wine
Hallelujahs, Hail Marys, hunger and plenty
Days of hurricanes and days of serenity

Tattoos of things I swore would never change
But each falls behind at the turning of the page.

My past self would've hated who I am today
And I still feel that hatred in the parts of him that stayed
I've changed so much and yet something's lacking
I still don't know how to accept being happy

I once thought I had every answer, full of hubris
But I never knew anything and now I'm still clueless
Each page testifies to truths that are now lies
Stories of sunny days read under cloudy skies
These pages are filled with the places I've been
The memories I've made and mysteries within.

MUSINGS

These thoughts are cancerous and poetry is chemo
Love is my slot machine and life my casino
Me versus myself, the score is still zero
This battle's bloodier than a film by Tarantino.

It's all gone to nonsense, it's a woozy, it's a wozzie
Drifting off mid-sentence like a verbal kamikaze . . .
Searching for myself, found you, but lost me
Love is priceless but that doesn't mean it's not costly.

A walking dichotomy of darkness and light
Trying to be successful just out of self-spite
Invisible thoughts blocking my sight
Smothering myself, in the hopes I'll ignite.

Firing on all cylinders, but I'm the squarest of all
Pushing against myself, Newton's third law.
Tape together shattered pieces, ignore the cracks and flaws
Emotion, like sushi, is best served raw.

THE ACTOR

Red curtains drape down from the ceiling
Lights ready, music, and so it begins
I step forward and whoosh, the curtains part
Like the red sea did for moses.
I speak with a voice, not mine
and with words I can't take credit for
If I portray this character well enough
The actor will be lost and the character remembered.
The love interest is introduced on stage
I declare my love for her with orchestrated feeling
The audience claps when we kiss, but I
Feel nothing, of course; it's just an act.
An emotional soliloquy follows,
and with it, conjured tears
We take our bows when the final act ends
The audience roars with approval;
They get up to leave at last and I,
I wash the stage makeup off, but look the same.
A fan comes up after the show,
and asks for my autograph
Oops, I've signed the character's name, not mine
But it doesn't matter, they're the same.
They think it's my modus operandi
But this performance is my magnum opus
Real life is just another stage.
Just another stage where I have to look and act
Like I have everything put together;
everything neat, perfect, and in order,

when in reality I'm slowly dying,
Slowly decaying, screaming and clawing,
at this little box I've been put into,
Trying desperately to escape.
I'm just a character, with my face, my name,
my voice, but the words that come out
of my mouth
were put there by others.
I fear that one day I will fall so deeply in character
That I will forget the person I one day wish
To find the courage to actually be.
The crowd screams for an encore;
Heart racing, pulse at machine-gun pace,
I step forward, ignoring the withering glares
of the other actors in this play we call life;
I step forward, and for this final act,
and all other acts, going forward,
For the encore and eternity, I promise to be
Myself.

I WANTED TO ASK YOU

I wanted to ask you
Whether you'd ever heard
A piece of music so beautiful,
That it shattered who you are
And glued the pieces back together
Into some beautiful new configuration;

I wanted to ask you, truly
But I did not have the courage
To look so deeply into your soul
In fear that I would, in doing so, find
Things in my own mind I had been hiding
From myself.

I wanted to ask you
What thoughts plague your mind
When you stay up past midnight
And allow your brain to think freely;
I wanted to know, truly I did so,
But I merely wanted, and did not do.

I wanted to ask you
Many a thing, telling it true
I wanted to delve into your soul
And find out what makes you, you;
I wanted to, but I guess I'll just settle
For a "I'm good, how about you?"

FINGERPRINTS

The ridges of your fingertips match
The ridges of my brain;
Every wavy, fossilized scratch
Is one and the same.

Like a handprint in cement
An indelible mark has been left
My identity has been bent
At the point where your fingers pressed.

Some people leave their marks
All over your identity;
Some leave beautiful art
And others graffiti obscenities.

Some plant sweet fruits
In the brain's plowed ridges
And the nefarious produce
Poisons and call them riches.

The dust of time reveals these crimes
Where marks were left in dark of youth
Look between these fingerprint lines
As night ends, light reveals the truth.

HONESTY IN WRITING

I find that lately
In the words I've been writing
I've been truthful
But not quite honest.

I've told of deep loves
Lasting scars, thoughts,
And my favorite brand
of candy bar, but
I've been holding back.

I haven't told the world
Of my inspirations,
my idols, my beliefs,
my values, my code,
I haven't been honest
About the whole person I am.

I've shown beauty, but
Held back the darkness, I've
Spoken loudly and dropped the mic
But refrained from quietest mumbles,

And truly I believe the difference
Is more important than you
might realize.

If I may dip into the philosophical;
The somewhat meandering,
But altogether more honest
Realm of existence, as it were;
I would say I've been showing
The world my art, but
I have not been showing the world
Who I am.

I've been writing in stanzas
As they reflect clean thoughts
But held back from the dirty,
messy, inappropriate, but
Entirely honest realm
of the things in life

That go against what you
might expect.

SELF-DIAGNOSIS

I've been worried since I left the womb
Like a schizophrenic on shrooms
Like a hypochondriac on crack
Never shy with the panic attacks;
Internal reality succumbs to psychosis
Dreams destroyed by self-diagnosis.

I've been alone since I learned to think
Like an alcoholic forced to drink
Like a gambler looking for jinx
Like a broke junkie huffing ink;
Fighting a battle where I've already been beat
I unchain my demons and let them speak.

"You were a failure before you first tried
Like a blank shot with no bullet inside;
You're an offbeat song with no melody
A brain surgeon born with leprosy
You will look upon a failed life and weep
Blood, brains, dirt; at last you'll sleep."

I have no response or retort
No defending lawyer in this court
Back against the wall, me versus them all
Fistfight my demons till one of use falls
I don't have possessions or methods to cope
Just some luck, this mind of mine . . . and hope.

GRAPHOLOGY

I wonder if future archaeologists
Will unearth these written works of mine
Handwritten, as always
And attempt to decipher
The person I was
Based on my handwriting.

Here we see he crosses his t's
About halfway, they might say
And his writing slants rightward
About fifteen degrees;
Might they think they've
Cracked my code
In all my complexities?

The swooping g indicates indecisiveness
And the looped l a sense of pride;
Gothic v's scream of dishonesty
And the sharp n tells of pain . . .
Is this splotch of water from tears
Or just rain?

Cryptographers may study me
And my writing for a day
Or a decade perhaps, though even then
The truth is equally far away.
Sadly, we have no control
Of what history will think
We were trying to say.

SADISTIC FICTION

I've always hated it when authors seem to find joy
In killing my favorite characters.
With gleaming eyes they toy
With turmoil in every chapter.

Just when they've got you attached
To the character's quirks and flaws
To their words and their demons
Just when you've fallen in love
With the character's identity—
With a cruel turn of the lip
The author smirks and kills them off
And at our gasped pleas, merely scoffs.

But the author was God
And my favorite character was you
And I still can't believe
You're gone.

WANDERING SOUL

I am a wandering soul
Looking for something more
I feel this constant pull
A longing I just can't ignore.

I've searched the rocks of mountains
I've knelt on cathedral stones
Sleepless nights by the thousands
Have left weariness in my bones.

Question marks are met with periods
By people full of arrogance
They have every answer, nothing mysterious
And yet they have no evidence.

Love and hate, yin and yang
Meditation, medication, therapy
Multiverse, strings, the big bang
It's all helplessness to me.

I am a wandering soul
Looking for truth and meaning
And though my life may never feel full
At least I find solace in searching.

UNCHARTED

I look upon a frigid, empty abyss
Filled with a million human beings
A city whose name is foreign to my tongue
And whose air reeks of cigarettes
Expelled from the lungs of many wayward souls
Each one hastening the coming of death
Seeking the end of fruitless searching.

We are each on our own quests
To find meaning in our lives
But the meaning we seek
Is only a reflection
Of everything we have lost before.

I look up at a dark ceiling.
Sleep is a lover
Who never arrives
When she promised she would
She offers no excuse for her lateness
But nonetheless her arrival is welcomed.

This is one of those nights
Where she has stood me up
For the thousandth time;
But my body betrays my hatred of her
And I give in to her demands
Like a ghost given to drunkenness.

I feel despair from deep in my soul
It is a well of constant outpouring;
Hope tempts from the other side
But it cannot be trusted
Because that's the thing about hope—
It's just despair with wings.
Truly, the worst kind of loneliness
Is not even having yourself
To stand by.

I look up upon a sparsely starred abyss
Having wandered to this street corner
In the middle of the night
Watching the cars and people go by
Wondering
If this deep, black nothingness
Is the sum total of being human.

KEEPING CREATIVITY

The composer Hans Zimmer once said
He felt that creativity was like
A faucet of running water
A source from somewhere else,
The origin of which was a mystery;

He said he was afraid that one day
The faucet would run dry
And this mysterious flow
Of talents, creativity, and love,
Would suddenly run out.

I, too, know this feeling—
I cannot identify within myself
The origin of talents.

But I am not afraid
of the day the faucet
runs dry.

I see it this way;
I have been given these many
talents, abilities, thoughts,
creativity, and so much more,
But they are not mine to keep!

No, they are given to me
So that I may return them to the world

Many, many times over;
Our light was not meant to be kept
To ourselves until it burns down
To ashes;
No.

Every spark of life we hold
Within ourselves,
we must fan
into a full flame that will
Find the dry, crusty ground
of a parched soul to be
fertile ground in which to plant
A self-multiplying crop of life,
But for every crop and new life,
first something old must die,
And I am willing for that something
To be everything I am.

I will know I have succeeded as a person
As an artist, as a human being
When I have nothing left to give;
When every poem, every story,
every melody, every song has been written;
When every photograph has been taken and hung,
When my ideas have all been brought to fruition,
When I sit down to write, and find
That the pen of creativity has run dry,
When the vitality of ink, my blood,
has been used up, when it has dried up,

and I find myself there, empty,
bereft of talent and ideas;
When I have nothing left to give,
I will be satisfied.

Because I don't want to look back
And think that I could've given more;
I could've pushed harder,
bent the universe just a bit further,
into a better shape, as I see it;
I will keep giving away this
living water
To thirsty mouths
Until, at last,
the faucet runs dry
And I am empty;
pure, clean, with
nothing left to give;
poured out, used up,
Even the dust of death
becoming a fertilizer
for the future.

So help me God, I will not die
Until the faucet has run dry.

DISABUSED NOTIONS

When I was six I was sure I would become an astronaut.
I would invent things and become president.

When I was nine I was sure I would design Legos all day.
I would be the next Willy Wonka, the King of sweet teeth.

When I turned ten I learned about death and suffering.
It turns out Santa's not real, or the Easter bunny, and more.

Disillusion hit me like a six-thousand-pound truck
Going seventy-five in a fifty zone, catastrophic.

All my childhood dreams, filled with hope and optimism
Dissipated like a fog under the pressure of mid-day sun
Beating down with a stern harshness and unflinching heat
Cauterizing these fresh wounds on my soul with a fierce fire.

There's a reason stories of hope are called stories;
The fiction label should be a bit more pronounced, I think.

I used to look forward to freedoms and making it big;
Now I just hope to make ends meet.

Disabused of all these notions of hope
What can you attain when your spirit's broke?

BENDING THE UNIVERSE

Steve Jobs said he wanted
To put a dent in the universe.

That is a statement that has inspired me
To want to bend it to my will.

People often ask me, do you want
To be the next Steve Jobs?
The next Walt Disney?
The next Einstein?
The next . . . and the list goes on.

No, no I do not.
I don't want to be 'the next' anybody.
But I will tell you one thing.
I'm going to bend this universe of ours
To such an incredible extent
That children in the future
Looking upon the stars to see their futures
Will say they want to be
'the next' me.

I hold no illusions as to my genius
Or lack thereof, in truth,
But I know anything is in reach
To those willing to go to any lengths

To get what they want.

Everest is a pebble, Marianas is a dip;
Compared to the sheer magnitude
Of the Universe, with its
Hundreds upon hundreds
of billions upon billions
of galaxies;

And with that perspective,
Do not take it lightly
When I say,
I will do whatever it takes
To get what I want.

I will bend the entire universe
If I have to
I will go to every length
If necessary
To mold this existence
To the shape I see fit.

Life wants to drown me under the waves
But I will rise once more, unscathed
As this charade of conformity goes ablaze
Be amazed as I rise from the haze.
Can't end my trajectory, it'll only be delayed
If it takes a second or a century, I'll still get my way.

ETERNITY

What does it take to please me?
How will I learn to be happy?
I could be the greatest things
And still yearn to be better
Because, in truth
My greatest fear on this earth
Is to be on my death bed
—Hopefully at an old age—
And to look back upon a life
That I didn't live to the fullest.

Even if I left behind a legacy
That would stand for a century
I would think of the length of history
And see that my contributions
To this planet of ours
Were nothing but a breath,
Nothing but a careless blink
Before the eyes of eternity
Refocus on something else
And I, forgotten.

The first things to disappear
After you've left this earth
Are the minute details,
The truly small things

That made up who you were.
Then it's the voice, the smile,
Then the eyes and face fade away,
And before long,
Only your name is left
Before even that disappears.

Maybe I feel this way
Because, growing up
I was taught that the
Only existence worth any
Consideration was eternal.
But eternity is a long time
And for now, what do I need
In order to not feel
Like I'm wasting my life,
Wasting this only opportunity?

Maybe happiness isn't for me;
Maybe I'm doomed to contemplate
The deep mysteries of existence
And leave the frolicking, the love,
The days in the sun to others.
But I hope that isn't the case.
I hope that one day
I will find rest
And will not worry
About these grand things.

THE WEIGHT OF THE FUTURE

I hope I end up one day
Having everything figured out
I hope I end up happy
Certain of what this is all about.

Pressure knocks at my door
A clock ticks and demands its due
The lava burns from the floor
But not in a game like it used to.

So little time to figure it all out
So many distractions to prevent success
I'm in a dark forest with no path or route
But this internal fire knows no rest.

I cry out and scream
Demanding answers, any at all
What does any of it mean
When will clarity call?

Darkness encroaches on vision
But ask for light and it blinds
Boiling distaste for indecision
Spills into this heart of mine.

Will I ever give my heart
To love without reservation?
Will I ever learn the art
Of waiting with true patience?

Am I even capable of loving
With more than an actor's grimace?
Will I ever stop juggling
My real self and my outer image?

When a blank page is a canvas
You are used to filling with words
Real life becomes stranded
As another canvas, the lines blurred.

Will I ever admit I need others?
Will I ever learn not to judge?
I hope I will go further
In the pursuit of giving love.

My hoping, my dreaming,
I lay them freely to die
I will be a present being
I vow to be truly alive.

SPECIAL PEOPLE

You're just one of those special people
You meet every once in a great while;

Those one-in-a-thousand souls
Whose eyes speak of galaxies
Whose soul speaks of mysteries
Whose breath whispers of freedom;

A free spirit
Whom the world could not keep locked up
In a prison of conformity;
I could speak of your honesty
For a century.

Someone so very real
They make everyone else
Look like pathetic facades
Too afraid to be anything
Or anyone
Close

To who they really are.

I could not begin to capture
The beauty
Of your soul
If I had a thousand pages
And a thousand days
To fill with words
Declaring how you amaze me.

You know who you are, kindred spirit
And I hope one day you read this
And smile, thinking of the time
When our souls grazed one another
Resulting in sparks of electricity;

I will keep you in my thoughts
And become just a little bit more
Like you
Because
You're just one of those special people
You meet every once in a great while.

CYNICAL

The music used to pulse through me
I could feel it in my bones
It shook my spine and gave me shivers
Oh, the music used to move me.

I used to watch a sad movie
And tear up at least a little bit
I might wipe the tear away in shame
But at least I felt something.

Where did those innocent summer days go?
When did cynicism sneak up and consume me?

I wish I could hear a sad story
And not dismiss it out of hand
Saying it is nothing more
Than a method of getting sympathy
From someone else.

I wish I could see butterflies burst from cocoons
Without tempering my amazement
Knowing all beauty eventually dies.

I drive alone up the mountains
Just so I can scream at the top of my voice
Hoping the loudness of that sound
Will rattle my bones as music used to
And I would awaken
From this stupor—
This cynical, deathly stupor.

I am buried alive
In a casket of my own doing
Someone please, someone please
Command me to come alive
Like Lazarus
And bring me forth
From this jaded tomb.

INTERNAL COMBUSTION ENGINE

Sometimes I miss the sadness.
It cut through the confusion
In some way it made me sharp
It made me somehow more than human
And put brilliance in my art.

Sometimes I miss the pain.
It was the fire burning the fuel
That was my hopes and dreams
And turned them from minuscule
Into power for this machine.

I made a deal with the devil.
God gave me seeds, soil, and light
Which I traded for a minstrel's guitar
Seeking money and power in new heights
Considering no self-destruction too far.

I wonder if I'll ever be satisfied.
I could watch this fuel burn
Or find some positive self-expression;
Before it eats me away I must learn
To create without using depression.

THE BOX

As a kid, I never was the type to color in the lines.
I used to wonder, why do the lines even exist?
When these pictures in my head are ripe for harvesting
And I can give the world something it's never seen before.
They said, "Think outside the box!"
But truly, I don't think they meant it.
Or perhaps they meant it literally, as in,
"Think outside the box, but stay inside it."
I don't think they much approved
of my incessant attempts to break free.
For once I had tasted freedom,
I resisted what I saw to be a prison cell.
Tired of my antics, they locked me in as I was daydreaming
And threw away the key with a laugh.
There I was, locked away in that roomy box,
So, I decided to have a look around.

A heavy, immovable, drab wooden desk
And on it, a form with checklists and neat little spaces
And next to that, a generic gray metal pen.
Behind the desk, an average-sized chair
With an average-sized headrest
Much too small for me, it appeared.
There was a rack of clothing near the back,
A row of black suits and white shirts;
As I walked past, I picked up the scent
of a generic male cologne drifting dully in the air.
I opened a desk drawer to see what was within.
A book, labeled "Vacation Photos!" In small, all-caps print.

Perhaps that would be of some interest . . .
I flipped it open casually, shifting in the rigid chair.
I expected pictures of sunny days, beach living, and fun,
But I did not find any.
Instead, there were black-and-white photos;
The subjects: a TV set, a worn-in couch,
and an at-home office.
Bored already, I turned my attention
to thoughts of getting out.

I tried the door, but it was barred with a heavy lock;
I looked for a window, but found only an empty frame.
"Let me out!" I screamed, banging loudly on the door.
"This is your home now, don't you see? This is your new life."
Was the muffled reply from the other side.
Already claustrophobic, I fell to my knees and wept.
"Don't be sad, there's plenty to like about the life
We've already got planned out for you.

"War is Peace, Freedom is Slavery, and Ignorance is Strength;
After some time, you'll love the box like a big brother.
We'll put you through twelve nice years of school
Where you'll learn to see this box as beautiful;
your memories of freedom and possibility will slowly fade
And you'll realize you don't really need to think for yourself.
After that you'll go to a college or university
In year multiples of two, four, six, or more
Where the dreams we've told you are acceptable to have
Will be narrowed down, categorized, and trained for
Until you're small enough to be a nice little worker bee.

"You'll sleep for eight hours, work for eight hours, and then
in the remaining eight hours, we have all sorts of screens,
gadgets, doodads, and pleasant toys for you to play with,
With just enough variation to keep you vaguely satisfied.
You'll have just enough rebellion in these first few years
To placate you into inaction until you die.

"After some time has passed, you'll feel it time to fall
into this crazy thing we call 'love'; but do, do of course
be very careful that you do so only as we have prescribed
And with the established pattern of how it is to be done.
You'll sign a paper and say some vows
And reproduce so the cycle can start all over again.
Then you'll retire comfortably, watching spectacle sports,
politics, and birds, until you die at long last
And we put you in an even smaller box, in neat rows,
with all the others who have their own little boxes, too."

I sat in stunned silence, seeing at last how the world worked.
Sadness overcame me, and I lamented this reality;
the fact is, for me, the box they wanted me to end up in
The one six feet under, nicely insulated, and made of wood,
Was the same one they wanted me to live in
For my entire life, from first breath to last.
There's not a thing wrong with the things in the box,
But the constraints of staying within it are killing me.
If it takes every single second of every day I have left
I will shatter this prison, and then I shall be free
at last.

section five

nature

SECTION V: NATURE

CONTENTS:

Life can only be so bad when the beauty
of nature is so abundant.

ABOVE THE CLOUDS

Way up in the mountains
Sea level too far to be seen
The clouds mask civilization below
People replaced by a sea of green.

Peace falls down from heaven
In the form of a cleansing rain
The trees could tell endless stories
If you knew how to hear what they're saying.

An ocean of gray spills out below
Walk on it if you dare to drown
Its tendrils reach out and the waves crash
But it all happens without a sound.

Above the clouds, below the stars
No money here, but endless wealth
Inward is the hardest adventure of all
Come above the clouds and find yourself.

THE SUN, THE MOON (A ROMANCE STORY)

The sun begins to crest the
Looming, mountainous facade,
Sending a cascade of golden light flittering through
The calm, yet swift river,
Making the whole scene
Come alive with
Golden hues.
This coronation of the day with a crown of
Golden spectacle and
Vibrant pageantry
Marks the end of the sun's
Slow waltz
Across the darkening sky.
The sun's lost dancing partner, the moon,
Would soon step out
Onto the dance floor
In search of her partner;
But this night, like every night spent in
Fruitless search
For millennia upon millennia,
The two lovers would find
No solace
In each other.

PASSING SEASONS

The sun charges into the mid-autumn night's sky
The frost melts away, everything comes alive
The birds chirp away in their orchestral reprise
But oh, they're in for an unexpected surprise.

The sun dances down below the horizon
The birds answer a call emanating from inside them
As the first snowflakes fall like tridents of Poseidon
We watch the seasons as they're written by God's pen.

Armies of snowflakes invade and combine with each other
Human beings flee from the site and take cover
This chill makes nature seem a most negligent mother
But the freest of spirits are those who aren't bothered.

Yes, we mourn the passing of our summer days
And adore a warm breeze in about a million ways
But if we cherish our Decembers as we do our Mays
We might learn some of what the snowflakes have to say.

TERMINATION DUST

Loose leaves tumble occasionally to the ground
Thick trunks wave gently in the breeze
But a shock awaits any of those who
Dare to look up past the trees.

Up, up, on the mountaintops
If you look up at this tectonic crust
Peer far, far into the distance
There, atop the mountains, is white dust.

A loud herald saying seasons are changing
The heavens deign to show their will, to speak
Look up, look up if you dare to find
A sprinkling of snow atop majestic peaks.

ROSEBUDS

A branch held on during the winter
Against countless winds and gusts
Armies of snow slowly retreated
The howling winds have been shushed.

Green attacks the canvas
And the scene is vibrantly alive
The birds return, the bees appear
To make honey in their hive.

Stalks flash up from the ground
But malicious weeds they are not
No, these are treasured rosebuds
Spreading beauty as nature ought.

The promise of much beauty
Brings bird songs to a halt
Rosebuds grow in perfect cadence
Dancing to life's slow waltz.

A BUTTERFLY, THE UNIVERSE

Every breath we take from the air
Takes oxygen from an insect's lungs mid-prayer
And every exhalation does loudly declare
That in the currency of life, we're millionaires.

A butterfly flapped its wings and Rome fell
A passerby's whistle cracked the liberty bell
And I dare urge the daring not to yell
Lest we so bid a skyscraper a rough farewell.

A snake's tongue slithered and man did sin
Let me tell you how the waves from a shark's fin
Did set the tides on D-Day and let the allies win;
Chance and destiny are identical twins.

A word was spoken and the earth created
Another phrase and the future was dictated
And so every action must be carefully weighted
We just never know how things are interrelated.

SEASON OF LOVE

The cool breeze kisses the green grass
Forgotten are the cold nights of winter past
Clouds paddle lazily across the summer sky.
Sunlight sighs down from above
So begins the season of love.

Fluttering eyes, the young testing their wings
They dance to the songs the chirping robin sings
Each one declares they are ready to fly.
Touch turns to kiss as night starts to fall
The season of love has dawned for all.

The stars and the moon smile on the scene
The cycle of renewal and newness it brings
They slip down the horizon as the hour draws nigh.
Morning brings sunrise and songs not yet sung
The season of love has only begun.

VOLCANO

Wisps of ashy, gray smoke flutter
From the peak of a mountain;
It appears Mother Nature has once again
Reneged on her promise
To quit smoking.

The earth shakes violently
Tectonic vibrations gyrate,
In a single moment a city could
Be buried in ashes
For eternity.

Flashes of orange, reddish light
Emanating from spewing lava;
This ancient formation has come alive
Back from dormancy
To burn the Earth.

UP THE MOUNTAIN ON A BRISK FALL DAY

The cracked, worn road curls away into the distance
The adjacent river blasts a loud symphony
If nature is a cathedral, this is the entrance
I walk in with an open mind.

Cars, voices, and smog fade away
As birds, squirrels, and the river take their place
I lose track of the date, what's today?
Only the sun can define it.

Snowcapped peaks look down from far above
But the nearby foliage is still green
Clouds embrace the mountains with love
As blue sky fades to pink.

A chill takes hold of the air
Animals scurry away for shelter
Snowflakes begin to fall, the earth will wear
A cloak of white tomorrow morning.

I ponder the meaning of nature's song
And why it weighs so on my heart
Alas, it is too cold, I must say so long
To this place of beauty, serenity, and peace.

A SEPTEMBER SUNSET

A fire burns in the evening sky
Breaking like an egg in a pan
A sea of yellowish orange spreads
In accordance with divine plan.

Vibrant paint drips to the edge
Of ashen clouds drifting past
The sun is a messy painter
Every brush stroke massive and vast.

The clouds are like matches
Starting as fiery flame
Then fading to ashes
A burning passion, tamed.

The red, orange, yellow leaves
On the ground in this season
Reflect the colors of the sky, and
The sunlight that used to feed them.

A September sunset beaming
Down as a sailor's last call
A herald for the coming winter
A message, enjoy the fleeting fall.

NOVEMBER'S NORTHERN LIGHTS

Lights dimmed, curtains opened wide
I can see clearly the view outside
We watch, curious and wide-eyed—
The beauty of Aurora's pride.

Green streaks dance across the sky
Red light joins, but bids a swift goodbye
Before coming back in a moment to retry
And join back in the dance way up high.

A billion stars beam in the background
They shout their stories without a sound
For their song is lost and drowned
By the symphony of lights, so profound.

City lights beam from across the lake
And join Aurora in the reflection to make
A blurred beauty which does so shake
Me to my senses, am I even awake?

This is the stuff of dreams and magic
Who knew nature could be this fantastic?
Who told these lights to be so enthusiastic?
A love letter from the sky, how romantic.

SNOWFLAKE

I always hear people say
That no two snowflakes are alike.

I've always wondered,
How do you know that?

Here, in my backyard,
Is a bunch of snowflakes
That nobody tested to see
If they were exactly the same
As any others.

So maybe there are
Many identical snowflakes.

Not that it matters, of course
They're beautiful either way.

A HUNDRED BILLION STARS

Innumerable pinpoints of light
Populate a sheer blackness
The stark contrast sends
Shivers down my spine.

What is it about this view
So vast and incredibly large
That magnifies our thoughts
Into equal proportions?

These many dots in the night sky
Like a giant connect-the-dots drawing
Are enough to drive one to believe
In the interconnectedness of all things.

When the brightness of one star
Is lost in the multitude of its brethren
It makes one feel so insignificant
But simultaneously irreplaceable.

Thoughts of chance and destiny
Burn into my retinas
So when I close my eyes
I see only profound thoughts.

Under a night's sky
Filled with a hundred billion stars
Is it so crazy to believe
Our paths were destined to cross?

Under a night's sky
So beautiful as this
The possibilities are endless
Fear melts into bliss.

THE DEATH OF SUMMER

Mountains fade to black
Silhouetted against the sun
The sunset loudly declares
That this day is done.

The stars are white pixels
The moon is but a sliver
I wish I could paddle away
In that constellation river.

But all beauty has an end
And glossy darkness brings the cold
The stench of death attacks the leaves
And green weakens its hold.

The rain that gave life in the day
Becomes icy snowflakes of chilly death
The grim reaper comes for the flowers tonight
And promises another day for the rest.

SKYDUST

Glimmering specks
Of the brightest dust
Against an abyss of darkness
The blackest of seas

As the hours tick by
The slowest of winds
Pushes these specks
Like hands of a clock.

They whirl and dance
Like electricity
Or monochrome lightning bugs
Against a noir field.

Each star, like our sun
Perhaps hosting a planet
Like ours, full of life;
Who can speak for infinity?

REQUIEM FOR A RAINDROP

Raindrops on flower petals
Are the sky's love letters
To the ground;

Each one is beautiful
Pure, clear, reflective
And full of passion.

Admire these letters up close
See how they use their surroundings
To better expound their contents.

They slip, full of motion
Refusing to be bound
And kept from new joy.

Some of these drops
Evaporated from Everest
And ended up at this spot;

A drop from the deepest ocean
Traversed on heavenly railway
To see its loved ones here again.

SUNRISE COFFEE

The rays of sun spilled
Like coffee into a pot
Gently, warmly flowing
Almost as an afterthought.

The morning dew melted to vapor
Rising into a morning mist
As the supple steam rose from the cup
And with the breeze, was dismissed.

I took my mocha with extra cream
As clouds drifted across the sky
Forming thick, bushy clumps
Becoming one with the liquid nearby.

I took my first sip
As sun crested horizon
The heat nearly burned my lips
As blue sky began to lighten.

I sighed with contentment
Enjoying the myriad flavors
The coffee swirled and mixed
Rhythmically as the light wavered.

AVENLIGHT

I often wonder
If we are so used to human communication
That we neglect the possibility
Of any other form
Outside of the ordinary.

Are we so arrogant as to believe
That our little wagging of floppy tongues
Against teeth and mouth
Which we use to move an alignment of neurons
(Which we call a thought)
From one organism to another
Is the only method of communication
In the entire universe?

Perhaps, for instance
That globulous fire organism
That we call the sun
Has been seeking to establish first contact
For millions of years
Cycling between the harsh ultraviolet
Of a desert sky day
And the avenlight glow
That comes just before sunset;
Struggling to crack the code
Of our meaningless flashes of city lights
In return.

The human eye can only see
So many colors;
I like to imagine
That when we look upon
A pitch-black night's sky
And ignorantly label it colorless
Is it actually filled with all the colors
We could never even imagine.

Perhaps all these imploding stars
Are missiles thrown between
Galaxies at war
And these spiral galaxies
Are merely winding up
For a punch
Ten billion years
In the making.

I often wonder and imagine
What lies just beyond the fringe
Of the human experience;
What is it that we do not see?

THE AUBURN SCENT OF PINE

The auburn scent of pine
Fills the autumn air
Birds chirp sorrowfully nearby
Hungover from the giddy of summer.

The sunrise leaps across the landscape
Like a child awoken from slumber
Ready to play and live with joy
Unaware of the impendingness of death.

Winter slashes her icy nails
Across the chalkboard of the seasons
The child has grown up a little now
And walks carefully, slowly.

Uneasiness, anxiety
Plague the movement of the light
As harsh darkness sets in
The child's light goes out.

The moon glares down on the scene
Like a decayed, hardened sun
Lively, gaseous nature
Deadened into wretched stone.

Long wilted leaves lie dead
Blackened by the weight of snow
Without light, does it even exist?
If there is no one left to see it?

The promise of rest is broken
As easily as an egg
And the light awakens
For the newness of spring.

As quickly as it began
The leaves fall from the trees
They have absorbed his light
But nonetheless fall again.

The auburn scent of pine
Fills the autumn air
The sun cringes, knowing
He will soon succumb to wintry despair.

I, FOREST

I am an ancient forest
Which has stood for a hundred thousand years
Bark has shielded countless rings
And time doth not remember my birth.

There are leaves on the outermost trees
Which swear that their fathers
Were nibbled upon
By the great Tyrannosaurus Rex.

But that predator faded away
And a new one took its place
The human, it was called,
And so our stories became intertwined.

I remember when Babylon fell
The story was told in whispers by our neighbors
And again when Rome did the same;
We heard the human stories with interest.

The stories fell silent after some time
And steam crept over the horizon
Our neighbors fell prey to the humans
And became the stuff of lodgings and markets.

A wave of fear overcame my trees
As the humans crept further outward
After a short while, they found me
And it was only a matter of time.

My extremities built their industry
And my middle built their warships
My trees heated their homes
Or sunk to the bottom of the ocean.

When I had dwindled, at last
The humans decided
That my oxygen breath
Did not merit a deadly fate.

But the cities spewed smog
And that monster demanded
More fuel, so that it could grow
To an infinite size, apparently.

Now I stand, the last one.
The proud, tough tree
With ten thousand rings
And as many stories to tell.

Then the fateful day came.
Chainsaws roared, and I
Was broken into pieces,
And the forest died.

No one counted my rings.
No one cared to ask
About the times that would
Truly amaze them.

No, the humans did not care.
Instead, I was scraped
Into many, many thin pieces
And on me, ink was printed.

Ten thousand copies were made.
Floatable barbecue!
Have a cookout while in your pool!
Fifty percent off at the supermarket!

I hope my death was worth it.
Now, they can cook in the pool
But I think they have forgotten
That they can starve of oxygen.

I was the most ancient of forests.
I saw the birth and death of nations
I saw the continents move
I watched life struggle.

Now I am ash and products.
Come get your floatable barbecue.
Perhaps the loss of my many rings
Was worth that occupied space on your shelf.

Thank you for reading this
collection of original poems.
If you liked this book, please
share it with others and/or
leave an online review to
help spread the word.

How This Book Came to Be

I never understood the appeal of poetry. I've always been a rather analytical, left-brained person, and I just never connected with what seemed to me to be over-exaggerated whining which people labeled "poetry."

That all changed when, in the seventh grade, I was assigned to do a poetry slam as a class assignment. Groaning with distaste, I decided my hatred of not succeeding in class outweighed my hatred of poetry, and the rest is history.

What I wrote at that poetry slam is, in fact, the first poem in this book, "Diversity." It was in writing and performing that piece that I discovered the power of words to affect how someone else sees the world. From then on, the idea of being able to transfer a feeling or idea from myself to another person has continued to fascinate me.

Validation of our own experiences is a fundamental aspect of being a human being. This is why we share so much and why social media even exists. It is human nature to share.

It is interesting to me that, if you overthink everything as I so often do, any form of performance inherently becomes absurd. What rational basis is there for someone to pretend to be another person and record it to make a movie? Why dress up in a silly costume and fake having emotions and experiences that are wholly manufactured by some writer who just decided that's what that person should portray?

The same goes for any form of music or comedy or anything else. If you really think about it, it doesn't make any sense. So on that level, it doesn't make sense for me to have written down these intensely personal ideas, feelings, and experiences which have originated within myself. Would it make any sense to publish a collection of equally personal medical notes from my physical self? Why is one an unquestioned societal norm and the other is an absurdity?

That's what comes of overthinking things. On a more pragmatic level, we do things simply because we do them. I wrote this book because I couldn't not write it. To stop myself from creating art would be as absurd as changing my personality and mannerisms entirely to become a wholly different person. I believe this applies to everyone in different ways.

Every second of every day, every one of us is creating something. We are creating moments. We are creating memories and feelings in the people around us, intentionally and unintentionally.

I find it interesting that by saying to someone "you just realized that you're breathing," you immediately cause them to go from breathing automatically and subconsciously to having to control their breathing manually and consciously. This is the power of words. It is a real, physical power—somehow, when we flop our tongues around in specific ways, audio waves are created that, when interpreted by the ears of another person, cause a real, physical change in that person such as I described above. I think that the effect our words have on the minds and probably the physical brains of others is magnanimously more powerful even than interesting little thought experiments such as the aforementioned.

This is why I am a writer. As I wrote in the poem "Fingerprints" in this book, everyone you come in contact with leaves some mark, however large or small, on your consciousness. Through the magic of the printing press and the fact that you have read this book, I am now one of those people, even though you more than likely don't know me at all.

That is my underlying philosophy of writing—the 'theory' of writing I espouse. The practical creation of the poems in this book, however, is a different matter.

The biggest component of writing, for me, is simply writing down every flash of inspiration you get during the day. Every one of those moments where you suddenly get an idea is a special one—they are each dots which you are subconsciously connecting into some greater picture with greater meaning. Writing them down solidifies them into the real world and, at the risk of sounding quasi-spiritual, shows your reverence and appreciation for those gifts of brilliance and ensures that more will keep coming.

I was inspired by the idea of method acting to go to extremes to write things that feel real. Method actors will often immerse themselves in the minutiae of their character and the character's life in order to give a stellar performance. I have endeavored to do the same in writing. This has ranged from actually finding a dusty attic with a piano for "Dust on This Piano" to writing most of the poems in the Nature section based on real locations in Alaska. At one point I stayed up for most of the night in the middle of nowhere with a pen and notepad in freezing weather one winter just so I could capture exactly what it felt like to see the northern lights on a perfectly clear night. While this probably wasn't necessary, I think there's some indescribable authenticity that this approach lends to creative work that is somehow always felt by the audience.

Many times, I just steal lines and ideas from my friends. For instance, the line "love gives the best of highs but the worst of hangovers" was stolen verbatim from something someone said to me, and serves as the crux of the story of the poem "Lithium." Almost every poem from the Love section contains elements from stories my friends have told me about their love lives—crushes, rejections, building, fading away, breakups, the aftermath. Stealing inspiration from my friends has allowed me to vicariously accumulate more experience from which to write poetry than I ever could on my own, and for allowing me to steal from their lives I am forever grateful to my friends.

The one place I couldn't steal inspiration from others for, however, was the Personal section. That required a great deal of introspection and trying to get to know myself as if I was another person. While I wrote about society because we are all part of it, love because we all feel it, nature because we all see it, and life because we all live it, I wrote about myself because I felt that this arc of life that I was attempting to convey through this book was incomplete without an intensely personal mark of my own inner self. This allowed this work to change from an almost clinical observation of completely outward events to an intensely personal sharing of life from myself to others, which is what I wanted to achieve.

When I had figured out the general topics I wanted to talk about, I had to decide what I wanted to talk about in each individual poem. I decided early on that I should limit this book in size so that it represented only the best of my work. I wrote over 400 poems for this book over five years (perhaps the majority written in the final year of the project in which I truly was certain I would make a book out of it) and so I still had an excess of poems to select from. The criterion I decided for whether a poem should make the cut was this: if this poem was the only thing I could say to a room of 2,000 people, would I still say it? This requirement forced me to create only the truest and highest-quality things I could create. I hope you loved it.

Photo: "The Wave" first written draft

Photo: The dusty piano that inspired "Dust on This Piano"

Photo: Scene that inspired "A Butterfly, the Universe"

Photo: Scene that inspired "The Death of Summer"

Photo by Jovell

ABOUT THE AUTHOR

Justin Wetch is an artist, poet, photographer, musician, pretentious egomaniac, and messy-haired fool from Palmer, Alaska. He originally self-published this book at the age of 19 while a freshman at the University of Alaska Anchorage. He enjoys artistic endeavors and connecting with people.

www.justinwetch.com

Follow me on Twitter & Instagram @JustinWetch

ABOUT THE ARTIST

Malachi Paulsen was born in Ketchikan and raised in Wasilla, Alaska. He currently lives in Plains, Montana. Malachi started drawing when he was about 12 years old, pursuing the art of realism. Artistic talent runs in his family. Along with drawing, Malachi is an avid health and fitness enthusiast. *Bending the Universe* is the first book Malachi has illustrated, at the age of 16. He enjoys creating life from paper and graphite and challenging himself to develop more eye for detail every time he picks up a pencil. Malachi uses drawing as an escape into worlds of complexity and beauty and makes them feel real on paper. Malachi enjoys artistic pursuits and hopes to pursue a career where he can use his incredible talents to make the world a more beautiful place.

Bending the Universe was originally self-published by Justin Wetch in December of 2016 (over 7,000 copies sold) until it was picked up and republished by Andrews McMeel Publishing in spring of 2018.